Original title:
Night Owl Insights

Copyright © 2024 Swan Charm
All rights reserved.

Editor: Jessica Elisabeth Luik
Author: Aron Pilviste
ISBN HARDBACK: 978-9916-86-463-0
ISBN PAPERBACK: 978-9916-86-464-7

Silent Galaxy

In the silent galaxy, where stars softly sing,
Whispers of the cosmos on a gentle wing.
Ethereal light dances in the night,
Harmonic echoes of celestial sight.

Planets rotate in a ballet grand,
Cosmic seas wash over starlit sand.
The silence speaks of mysteries and lore,
Infinite skies with tales to explore.

Void of sound, yet full of grace,
Nebulas dream in the stellar space.
Invisible threads of the universe spin,
In the silent galaxy where it all begins.

As the Night Unfolds

As the night unfolds its velvet shroud,
The moon appears from behind a cloud.
Shadows lengthen under starlit sky,
Dreams take flight where spirits lie.

Whispers carried on the evening breeze,
Stories of old among the trees.
Lanterns flicker in the widow's way,
Hope entwines with the end of day.

Constellations cast their ghostly spell,
Tracing paths where angels dwell.
As the night unfolds, so too do we,
Writing our fate by destiny's decree.

Dusk's Intuition

Dusk arrives with a whispered hush,
Painting skies with a twilight blush.
Day retreats, yielding to night,
Stars ignite with ancient light.

Intuition whispers secrets old,
Mysteries watched, but never told.
The horizon fades, a gentle sigh,
Time suspended in the evening sky.

In the quiet, hearts find their beat,
In dusk's embrace, where shadows meet.
Wisdom blooms in twilight's glow,
Guiding souls where dreams may flow.

Serenades to the Moon

A crescent smile pierces night
with soft whispers of silver light.
Stars dance in celestial tune,
drawing breath from the sighing moon.

Oceans ripple in soft caress,
mirror waves, in moon's finesse.
Embrace silent, cool night's hue,
under the moon's serenades true.

Whispers travel across the sky,
carried on a breeze's sigh.
Luminous verses, whispers croon,
serenade the lonely moon.

Secret Nocturnes

Shadows cast in silver sheen,
murmurs of the night's serene.
Moonlight falls on whispered ground,
secret nocturnes all around.

Trees sway in the midnight mist,
each leaf touched by Luna's kiss.
Silent hymns by night composed,
in the dark, our dreams enclosed.

Mystery cloaked in dark attire,
whisper secrets, hearts' desire.
Twilight tales in shade cocooned,
piano notes, the night attuned.

Midnight Reflections

Glimmering on a tranquil sea,
midnight whispers call to me.
Reflections of a silvered moon,
dance upon the night's dark tune.

Windows hold the night outside,
whispers of the stars confide.
Silent echoes, deeply wound,
by the moon's spell all around.

Life reflected in starlit pools,
midnight's quiet, gentle rules.
In the calm, our spirits rise,
watched by countless, silent eyes.

Veil of Midnight

Veil of midnight softly drapes,
night unfolds with gentle shapes.
Stars above in silent flight,
guardians of the whispering night.

In the quiet, worlds unite,
underneath that velvet light.
Ethereal glow, shadowed croon,
bathed in the embrace of the moon.

Silent dreams in twilight bound,
mystic journeys, night astound.
Through the veil, a world reborn,
night descends 'til morn is sworn.

Beyond the Midnight Veil

In shadows deep, where whispers trail,
Lies the realm beyond the midnight veil.
Where moonlight dances, dreams entwine,
Secrets of stars in silence divine.

A silver glow, so soft and pale,
Guides the way with a gentle sail.
Through the vast expanse, endlessly frail,
Echoes of time, eternal tale.

Mysteries seep through every fold,
Night's chiffon, woven bold.
Beyond the veil, where stories are told,
Lies a world, timeless and old.

Thoughts of the Twilight

Twilight whispers with colors bright,
Blending day and encroaching night.
Thoughts cascade like the evening light,
Painting dreams in hues so slight.

Moments pause, the world so still,
As shadows creep over the hill.
In twilight's glow, minds softly fill,
With musings deep, a gentle thrill.

The sun dips low, horizons blur,
With twilight thoughts, hearts confer.
Between the day and night's allure,
Dreams are born, pure and demure.

Silent Stars Speak

Silent stars in a velvet sky,
Whisper secrets as they fly by.
In their glitter, stories lie,
Ancient tales we can't deny.

Their light penetrates the deepest night,
A beacon for the wanderer's sight.
Silent stars in their silent flight,
Sing a song, soft and bright.

Galaxies dance, a cosmic spree,
In the vastness, lost are we.
Yet silent stars, in their decree,
Speak of wonders, wild and free.

Unbroken Stillness

In the hush of night, an endless sea,
Unbroken stillness, wild yet free.
Whispers of the wind, a symphony,
Nature's breath, in perfect harmony.

The world sleeps, wrapped in dreams,
Unbroken stillness, it softly gleams.
Time stands still, or so it seems,
A moment's pause in life's swift streams.

Amidst the calm, hearts find peace,
In unbroken stillness, worries cease.
The night unfolds with gentle ease,
A soothing silence, sweet release.

Mysteries Under the Moon

Whispers of shadows dance, so bright,
Veiling the truth in silken night.
Glow of the moon, an ethereal boon,
Guiding through realms of hidden light.

Crickets serenade, melodies thin,
Stories unfold, where dreams begin.
Echoes of ages, secrets in sand,
Unraveling myths with a gentle hand.

Stars sprinkle tales, cryptic, profound,
Lost in the silence, meanings unbound.
Wisps of the past, future in tune,
Revel in mysteries under the moon.

Night's canvas painted, dark and serene,
Hues of wonder, seldom seen.
In the moonbeam's tender embrace,
Timeless enigmas leave their trace.

Midnight Epiphanies

Under the cloak of midnight skies,
Thoughts awaken, wisdom flies.
Moments of clarity, pure and clear,
Born in silence, no one hears.

Mystic winds whisper through trees,
Truths revealed with gentle ease.
Dreams align with ancient lore,
Midnight's epiphanies explore.

Moonlit paths, reflections deep,
Secrets out where shadows creep.
In the quiet, insight blooms,
Epiphanies in calm, dark rooms.

Stars align, a cosmic dance,
Minds unfold in their trance.
Whispers gathered, spirits free,
Crafting midnight's epiphany.

Subdued Reflections

Beneath the twilight's soothing hue,
Reflections come, serene and true.
Past and present in a tender blend,
Mellow thoughts on whispers send.

Gentle ripples on a placid lake,
Memories stirred, the heart they wake.
Subdued musings softly gleam,
In the dusk's gentle, amber beam.

Silent echoes of a bygone day,
Unfolding softly, in muted ray.
Thoughts like leaves, adrift, content,
Subdued reflections, time well spent.

Evening blends with thoughts so mild,
Nature's verse, unhurried, wild.
In these quiet, placid sights,
Reflections find their tranquil nights.

Starlight Soliloquies

Under the vast and twinkling sheen,
Stars converse in a silent scene.
Solitude's sweet serenade,
In twilight's tender, cool cascade.

Thoughts as bright as the Northern Star,
Murmur softly, near and far.
Lonely hearts and wistful dreams,
Adrift in starlight's gentle streams.

Cosmic tales, in glitter spun,
Each a soliloquy begun.
With every shimmer, distant voice,
In stardust whispers, thoughts rejoice.

Celestial dance on velvet night,
Lonely musings find their light.
In the hush of cosmic seas,
Whisper starlight soliloquies.

Awake in Moonlight

Silver beams caress the night,
Tender whispers in their flight.
Leaves rustle a quiet tune,
Underneath the mystic moon.

Stars ignite the velvet skies,
Glimpse of dreams in weary eyes.
Softly, shadows start to dance,
In the glow of moonlit trance.

Silent beauty, pure and vast,
Moments drift but never last.
Night's embrace, a gentle sway,
Guiding dreams till break of day.

Murmured Dreams

Soft winds carry whispered tales,
Of hidden paths and moonlit trails.
Lulled by whispers, shadows creep,
Into the heart of murmured sleep.

Echoes of the night's allure,
Blend with dreams so calm and pure.
Crickets sing a lullaby,
Underneath the twinkling sky.

Nighttime's breath, a soft embrace,
Dreams take flight at gentle pace.
In the quiet of the night,
Hope and peace in dreams alight.

Ethereal Shadows

Shadows dance in ghostly light,
Silent phantoms of the night.
Mystic figures softly glide,
In the moon's ethereal tide.

Whispers from the dark unknown,
Voices in the twilight zone.
Veiled secrets of the past,
In their glow, will shadows cast.

Through the night, a story spins,
With the rise of midnight winds.
Dreams awaken, boundless flight,
In the realm of shadowed light.

Heavenly Solitude

Stars above in vast array,
Silent guardians of the gray.
Peaceful night, a tranquil sea,
Wraps the world in harmony.

Whispers in the still of night,
Guide the heart towards the light.
Lonely, yet so deeply blessed,
In solitude, the soul finds rest.

Dreams unfold beneath the stars,
Healing all our earthly scars.
In this quiet, pure and true,
Heaven's peace refreshes you.

The Owl's Gaze

In twilight's deep embrace, an owl does soar,
With feathered wings, it whispers ancient lore.
Silent in flight, beneath the moon's soft blaze,
The world is still, under the owl's gaze.

From lofty perch, it watches shadows play,
As dusk descends and night consumes the day.
Its eyes, like lanterns in the starlit maze,
Reveal the secrets lost in twilight's haze.

The forest wakes, nocturnal symphony,
An owl's call, a soulful melody.
Through woods and fields, its silent path it lays,
Guardian of night, under its wise gaze.

Embers in the Night

The campfire's glow, a beacon ever bright,
In darkened woods, it casts a warm respite.
Embers dance with stories soft and light,
Whispers of dawn, hidden from our sight.

Beneath the stars, we gather close and near,
Old tales resound, released from time's veneer.
The crackling logs, the heart of this delight,
Our spirits rise with embers in the night.

A hush descends, as night takes gentle hold,
The fire's warmth, a comfort to the bold.
In flickered beams, the forest feels less slight,
Dreams take flight with embers in the night.

Ode to the Stars

Across the velvet sky, stars softly gleam,
Each one a beacon for a sailor's dream.
Constellations weave their timeless art,
A dance of light that captivates the heart.

Beneath their glow, the earth feels small and still,
A universe, a vast and boundless thrill.
With every spark, a story to impart,
Our hopes and fears tied to their brilliant chart.

The Milky Way, a river made of light,
Guides wayward souls through darkness of the night.
In silence deep, where ancient starlight streams,
We find our peace in interstellar dreams.

Serenades Past Sunset

When daylight fades, and twilight takes its place,
The evening air is filled with soft embrace.
A symphony of whispers, cool and light,
Serenades that usher in the night.

The nightingale begins its soulful tune,
Under the watchful eyes of crescent moon.
Its melody, a beacon in the dark,
Hearts respond to every gentle spark.

Beneath the canopy of twinkling stars,
Our dreams and longings feel less like scars.
In this tranquil hour, the world seems right,
Lost in serenades past sunset's light.

Dusk to Dawn

Shadows stretch as day retreats,
Whispers of the night arise.
Stars ignite in silent feats,
Moonlight dances through the skies.

Crickets sing their twilight song,
Cool breeze sways the ancient trees.
Dreams awaken, soft yet strong,
Lost in nighttime's gentle seize.

Hours drift on velvet tides,
Secrets whisper from afar.
Midnight's chariot smoothly glides,
Guided by the northern star.

Restless thoughts in quiet sound,
Journey through the pulsing night.
Til the golden rays are found,
Dawn bestows its morning light.

Glimmers in the Gloom

Deep within the forest's heart,
Glimmers find their gentle way.
Luminous they slowly start,
Chasing shadows where they lay.

Spiderwebs in moonlit dew,
Sparkle with ethereal gleam.
Radiance in shades of blue,
Echoes of a distant dream.

Glow from wings of fireflies,
Twinkle through the ancient night.
Softly, gently, they arise,
Casting halos pure and white.

Mystic light in darkened halls,
Whispers from the past appear.
In the gloom, the spirit calls,
Illuminating what is near.

Under the Midnight Sky

Beneath the vast and starlit dome,
Whispers of the cosmos near.
Echoes from the void we roam,
In the glow, the dreams appear.

Planets dance on velvet threads,
Tracing arcs of time and grace.
While the universe outspreads,
Infinite in night's embrace.

Constellations weave their tales,
Stories of the ancient lore.
Silent whispers on the gales,
Resonate through evermore.

Ephemeral is the dance,
While beneath the stars we lie.
In their glow we find a trance,
Bound under the midnight sky.

Celestial Meditations

In the still and silent space,
Hearts and minds commence to drift.
Dreams align in pure embrace,
As the cosmic veils lift.

Planets hum their ageless notes,
Harmonies of cosmic birth.
Stars align like ancient quotes,
Scattered 'cross the endless girth.

Nebulae in colors rare,
Blossom with a mystic glow.
Beauty found in distant air,
Radiance from long ago.

In this quiet, souls converge,
Find their peace in astral light.
Meditative thoughts emerge,
Wandering the celestial night.

Stars as Witnesses

Underneath the twilight gleam,
We trace the paths of old,
Stars above, they watch our dreams,
In stories yet untold.

Silent sentinels of night,
They shimmer, bright and bold,
Bearing witness to our plight,
In whispers soft and cold.

Cosmic tales they softly sing,
Of love and ancient wars,
Their lights on timeless journeys wing,
Across the heavens' shores.

In their gaze, our secrets hide,
Amidst the cosmic sea,
Stars as witnesses, our guide,
In nights' tranquility.

Through their glow, we find our way,
In darkness, we are free,
Under stars, our hearts convey,
A silent, endless plea.

Awake in the Dark

When shadows fall and night descends,
My heart begins to race,
In solitude, my soul contends,
With thoughts I dare not face.

Awake, I lie in silent fear,
Beneath the moon's embrace,
Whispers soft yet drawing near,
In dark's forbidden space.

The world outside is still, serene,
Yet restless is my mind,
In darkness, truths I've never seen,
Seek, and they will find.

Stars beyond my window pane,
Twinkle with a hidden spark,
Comforting my silent pain,
As I'm awake in the dark.

In this quiet, sacred hour,
Where shadows softly mark,
The boundaries of silent power,
Of being awake in the dark.

Nocturnal Whispers

In the quiet of the night,
Voices softly stir,
Nocturnal whispers taking flight,
In dreams that once were pure.

They dance upon the midnight breeze,
With secrets left untold,
Through the dark, their echoes tease,
With stories brave and bold.

Beneath the moon's ethereal light,
Their murmurs gently rise,
Whispers that ignite the night,
With soulful, sweet replies.

In shadows, they entwine their tune,
A symphony of yore,
Nocturnal whispers, ever boon,
To hearts that long for more.

These quiet tendrils of the dark,
Weave tales of love and woe,
In nocturnal whispers, hark,
The secrets they bestow.

Celestial Thoughts

In the calm of night, my mind does wander,
To realms beyond our sight,
Celestial thoughts, they grow fonder,
Beneath the spectral light.

Where galaxies spin tales of wonder,
And stars in silence speak,
Thoughts like whispers softly thunder,
In the vast cosmic creek.

Infinite journeys they embark,
Through time and endless space,
Celestial thoughts, they leave their mark,
In the night's quiet grace.

With every twinkle, they descend,
Upon my seeking heart,
In celestial thoughts, I transcend,
And from this world, depart.

In night's embrace, my spirit sails,
Through visions grand and wrought,
Guided by the cosmic trails,
Of my celestial thoughts.

Evening Ruminations

The sky ablaze with hues of gold,
Whispers of dreams yet to unfold.
In twilight's gentle, warm embrace,
The day's ambition leaves no trace.

Birds retreat to nests of care,
Stars peeking through the tranquil air.
Soft murmurs of a waning light,
Guide us gently into night.

Questions linger in the breeze,
Carried with the autumn leaves.
Hopeful hearts and weary eyes,
Silently they fantasize.

Moments cast in amber glow,
Hidden secrets start to flow.
Beneath the sapphire velvet sky,
Our silent thoughts begin to fly.

The evening winds sing lullabies,
To dreams that rise and touch the skies.
In the stillness, peace is found,
As night wraps tightly all around.

Shadowed Thoughts

In shadows deep where secrets lie,
Midnight whispers softly sigh.
The heart's confessions, all unseen,
In the silence flow serene.

Fears and doubts, a ghostly dance,
Glimmer in the moon's soft trance.
Unvoiced sorrows, dreams unwept,
In the shadows are they kept.

Echoes of the mind's deep well,
In the dark their stories dwell.
Shadowed thoughts, both old and new,
Paint the night in somber hue.

Lonely stars bear silent witness,
To the heart's profound stillness.
Each secret shadow, each dark trace,
Found within this timeless space.

Nighttime brings its own reflection,
Deep within, a dark connection.
Shadowed thoughts, a mute parade,
In the night, their truths displayed.

Moon's Embrace

The silver wheel ascends the night,
Bathing all in gentle light.
Its tender glow, a soft caress,
On weary souls, bestows finesse.

Guiding hearts through night's abyss,
Moonlight whispers of secret bliss.
Dreamers' canvas, vast and bright,
In the moon's embrace, take flight.

Reflections on the water's face,
Trace the moon's celestial grace.
Silent stories come alive,
Underneath its watchful eye.

Night's cool breath, a soothing balm,
Encounters weary souls with calm.
Softly healing, tenderly,
In the moon's embrace, we see.

In shadows cast by moonlight's glow,
Hidden realms begin to show.
A sacred dance through time and space,
Within the moon's gentle embrace.

Echoes in Moonlight

Moonlight's whispers softly trace,
Shadows in their silent chase.
Echoes drift on evening's breath,
Distant memories' soft bequeath.

Stars reflect their ancient tales,
In the air, an echo sails.
Haunting beauty fills the night,
With echoes bathed in silver light.

Nighttime's silence amplifies,
Echoes of the past arise.
Moonlight's glow, so pure and bright,
Gently lifts these echoes' flight.

Frozen moments come to play,
In the echoes of the grey.
Time stands still in moonlit haze,
Echoes dance in mystic phase.

In the quiet, still and deep,
Echoes through our spirits seep.
Moonlit path where shadows blend,
Echoes in moonlight never end.

Veiled Mysteries

In twilight's glow the whispers weave,
Through tangled woods where shadows cleave,
Ancient secrets trees conceal,
Beneath the branches, truths reveal.

Moonlight dances on the leaves,
Silent stories it retrieves,
Through mist and night, the past is clear,
Veiled mysteries, drawing near.

The whispered winds their tales impart,
A language old, it moves the heart,
Softly spoken, time's own hues,
In forests deep, with twilight views.

Heed the murmur of the trees,
In their cadence, find the keys,
Unlock the past, embrace the night,
Where mysteries dwell beyond our sight.

In veils of dreams, the night unfolds,
Ephemeral, these truths it holds,
Seek the silence, hear the call,
In twilight's arms, discover all.

Heartbeats of Darkness

In the quietude of night,
Shadows dance in pale moonlight,
Heartbeats echo, deep and slow,
In realms where only shadows go.

Stars above in dark embrace,
Twinkling in the silent space,
Darkness wraps the world in sleep,
Secrets in its bosom keep.

Heartbeats whisper, soft and low,
Mysteries we yearn to know,
In the stillness, find the way,
Through the shadows, night and day.

Silent footsteps through the dark,
Leave no trail, ignite a spark,
In the calm, the truth appears,
Guided by forgotten fears.

Embrace the night, its quiet breath,
In heartbeats, life defies the death,
In darkness, find a guiding star,
In every heartbeat, near and far.

Nocturnal Ponderings

Silent stars, they watch and gleam,
In the quiet, thoughts convene,
Whispers float on midnight air,
Questions rise without a care.

In the stillness, minds take flight,
Wandering through endless night,
Dreams conspire in hidden nooks,
Nighttime thoughts like ancient books.

Moonlight spills on tranquil ground,
In its glow, lost thoughts are found,
Musings fly on silver wings,
In the night, the soul it sings.

Quiet moments stretched in time,
Nocturnal ponderings, oh so fine,
Time unfolds its veiled hand,
In the dark, we understand.

As the night begins to fade,
Thoughts retreat, the dreams they've made,
In silence, wisdom softly stirs,
Nocturnal ponderings, profound and pure.

Celestial Quietude

Beneath the sky, in silent awe,
Stars above, no flaw, no flaw,
Celestial quietude holds sway,
Guiding hearts in night's ballet.

Softly speaks the night to me,
In its vast tranquility,
Endless reaches, starlit dreams,
In the quiet, wisdom gleams.

Galaxies in still repose,
In their silent, graceful shows,
Tracing stories on the void,
In the quiet, hearts are buoyed.

Starlight whispers ancient lore,
In the calm, we yearn for more,
Echoes of the cosmic tune,
In the night, our spirits swoon.

Beneath the heavens, vast and grand,
Celestial quietude, we understand,
In the silence, time suspends,
In the stars, our journey ends.

Wisdom in the Dusk

As day fades to gentle night,
Shadows weave their silent lore,
Ancient whispers take their flight,
Tales of yore, forevermore.

Twilight's grace, a purple dream,
Mysteries in hues that blend,
Time's soft hand reveals the seam,
Where beginnings meet their end.

Whispering winds convey the sound,
Of truths the dark skies bemoan,
Wisdom in the dusk is found,
In solitude, not alone.

Each star, a teacher, wise and true,
Lights the path we seek to know,
Through the stillness, visions grew,
Like a seed in dusk's soft glow.

In the quiet of the eve,
Minds awaken, hearts believe,
Night's embrace, we gently receive,
And in the dark, we find reprieve.

Reverie Under Stars

Beneath the vast, unending skies,
A sea of quietude unfurls,
In the still night, dreams arise,
In this realm of pearl-lit whirls.

Stars, like diamonds, pierce the veil,
Silent echoes from afar,
In their light, we hear the tale,
Of ancient, wandering stars.

Softly, softly, the night speaks,
Whispers of celestial grace,
Where the cosmos gently tweaks,
The threads of time and space.

Lulled by night's eternal gaze,
Hearts and minds begin to soar,
Wandering through the astral maze,
Infinite and evermore.

In the tranquil night, we find,
Thoughts merge with the cosmic sea,
Under stars, our souls unbind,
To embrace infinity.

Otherworldly Murmurs

Beyond the veil of drifting clouds,
Where silence reigns, a soft caress,
A realm unknown, where quiet shrouds,
The whispers of the universe.

Through the ether, voices speak,
Murmurs from the unseen crest,
In the quiet night they seek,
Eager hearts to manifest.

Mystic winds begin to weave,
Tales of wonder, sad and bright,
Otherworldly murmurs grieve,
For the lost, eternal night.

Stars align in patterns true,
Guiding those who choose to hear,
Wisdon in the night's soft hue,
Dissolving every earthly fear.

In the dance of shadows deep,
Hidden truths in whispers sleep,
Otherworldly secrets keep,
In our dreams, those voices seep.

Astral Contemplations

Gazing up at cosmic heights,
Souls embark on thoughtful quests,
In the tapestry of nights,
Universe within us rests.

Planets swirl in silent dance,
Nebulas like dreams unfold,
In this astral somber trance,
Time's deep mysteries behold.

Contemplating stars afar,
Wisdom in their ancient burn,
Every twinkle, every scar,
Lessons from the stars we learn.

Comets blaze with fleeting light,
Celestial wonders, fierce and brief,
In their trails, we see the sight,
Of our triumph and our grief.

Through the boundless cosmic sea,
Wander minds in contemplation,
Finding in eternity,
Moments of pure revelation.

Starry Night Reflections

Beneath the velvet evening sky,
Eternal whispers softly sigh,
Stars above in cosmic flight,
Reflections dance in tranquil night.

Glistening jewels in a dark expanse,
Their radiant light begins to prance,
Sending forth a dreamy gleam,
Casting shadows in a midnight dream.

Night's embrace, a sacred calm,
The universe hums a timeless psalm,
Each star a tale of endless lore,
A waltz of light forevermore.

Galaxies spiral, infinite and grand,
In orbits spun by unseen hand,
A tapestry of cosmic art,
Woven threads of human heart.

Silent echoes through the void,
Mysteries laid bare and unalloyed,
Bathed in dusk's celestial glow,
In starry night, we come to know.

Contours of the Dusk

As day departs in softened hue,
Shadows stretch and sky turns blue,
Contours form on twilight's crest,
A gentle calm, a time for rest.

Silhouettes of trees align,
Defining edge 'gainst dusk's design,
In the glaze of evening's light,
A transition 'tween day and night.

Amber skies and lavender fade,
Nature's palette deftly played,
Contours blur as darkness nears,
A symphony for sight and ears.

Whispers of a cooling breeze,
Sway the branches, rustle leaves,
Nightfall drapes the earth in silk,
A canvas of nocturnal ilk.

Stars arise in muted gleam,
Joining dusk in evening's theme,
Contours meld in twilight's clasp,
Night assumes its tranquil grasp.

Somber Stars

Glimmering through a heavy shroud,
Stars appear, serene yet proud,
In the quiet of the night,
They shine a melancholic light.

Silent echoes, whispers deep,
Secrets that the heavens keep,
Every point a distant dream,
A soliloquy in cosmic scheme.

Twilight journals in the dark,
Embers of a dying spark,
Somber stars in silent rows,
Bearing tales of ancient woes.

Curtains drawn on day's old stage,
This celestial, endless page,
Somber stories, softly spun,
Under the watch of a listless sun.

Grains of sand, in time's embrace,
Fleeting glimpses of a space,
Somber stars, eternal, cold,
In the vastness, truths unfold.

Interludes with the Moon

Moonlight's tender silver gleam,
Illuminates the quiet stream,
A celestial dance unfolds,
In melodies the night beholds.

Underneath the moon's embrace,
Whispers weave through time and space,
Interludes of light and shade,
Patterns in the evening made.

Reflections in the water's kiss,
Mirroring the lunar bliss,
Moon and earth in soft commune,
Interlude with graceful tune.

Night absorbs the gentle glow,
As moonlight sets the world aglow,
Intertwined in nightly trance,
A stellar circle does advance.

In the quiet of the night,
Moon presides in tranquil light,
Interludes with sky and sea,
Moments born in harmony.

The Midnight Muses

When silence cloaks the restless night,
Dreams embark on whispered flight.
Stars entwine with shadows deep,
Secret tales in moonbeams steep.

Underneath the sable sky,
Muses weave where echoes lie.
Thoughts unspoken, hearts revealed,
In the darkness, truth unsealed.

Songs of past and future blend,
In twilight's arms, the lines extend.
Whirls of wonder, tendrils light,
Dancing softly out of sight.

Night's embrace, a gentle guide,
Leading where our dreams reside.
Moments whisper, swift and fleet,
Muses' chorus, bittersweet.

As dawn prepares its golden crest,
Midnight muses find their rest.
Words now linger, softly drawn,
Till the night brings them to dawn.

Whispers of the Evening

Golden hues at twilight's end,
Where dusk and daylight gently blend.
Whispers shared on breezes soft,
Lull the weary, raise aloft.

Shadows lengthen, stretch and sway,
Mark the close of fleeting day.
Crickets sing their ancient tune,
Harmonize with crescent moon.

Veils of silver cross the sky,
Stars emerge as night draws nigh.
Each one tells a silent tale,
In the dark, where dreams set sail.

Trees stand tall, their whispers low,
Guided by the moonlight's glow.
Leaves a-rustle, secrets keep,
Guarding stories while we sleep.

Evening's song, a gentle spell,
In its magic, hearts do dwell.
Whispers of the night, they sing,
Of the peace that dusk does bring.

Midnight Contemplations

Hours late, the world in quiet,
No more day, and no more riot.
Softly ticks the clock's old hand,
Pausing, time's long stretch withstand.

Candles flicker, shadows play,
In this midnight's soft ballet.
Thoughts meander, minds unwind,
Paths of past and future twined.

Wisps of memories arise,
In the stillness, no disguise.
Moments lost and dreams held close,
Hidden where the moonlight glows.

Questions echo, answers lie,
In the dark, beneath the sky.
Contemplations deep and vast,
In the present, future, past.

Morning whispers on the brink,
Stars begin their final blink.
Midnight's musings softly cease,
As the dawn restores its peace.

Moonlit Musings

Silver streams of moonlight pour,
Casting patterns on the floor.
Silent whispers, echoes bright,
Fill the stillness of the night.

Thoughts take flight on lunar beams,
Drifting softly in our dreams.
Far-off places, hearts' desires,
Glimmer in the moon's soft fires.

Breezes gentle, night air clear,
Wrap around with tender cheer.
Stars above in silent gaze,
Mark the pathways of our ways.

In the glow of moon's embrace,
Find a sweet and gentle grace.
Time stands still, and hearts find peace,
Underneath the silver fleece.

When the dawn begins to climb,
Ending moments out of time,
Moonlit musings fade from view,
Till the night returns anew.

Luna's Reflection

In night's embrace, she gleams so bright,
A silver crescent in the sky,
Whispering secrets through the night,
As stars around her gently sigh.

She waltzes through the darkened shroud,
A tranquil dance above the earth,
Her light, a beacon through the cloud,
Reveals the night's celestial worth.

Soft echoes of her ancient love,
Echo across the midnight seas,
Reflecting in the waves above,
A symphony of whispered pleas.

With every phase, her tale unfolds,
A cycle timeless, ever new,
The moon, in silence, gently holds,
The dreams that weave the night in blue.

When dawn arrives and shadows flee,
Her glow fades to the morning light,
But in the heart of memory,
Luna's reflection stays in sight.

Afternoon of the Moon

As daylight wanes, the shadows grow,
A hidden world begins to wake,
Beneath the twilight's gentle glow,
The moon prepares her silent stake.

In the fading warmth of the sun,
She waits behind the azure veil,
A silver orb, her journey begun,
To tell the stars a wistful tale.

Her presence softens evening's fall,
A guardian of the coming night,
She rises slow, her glory small,
Yet powerful, her softest light.

The world beneath begins to dream,
Bathed in her ethereal hue,
Night creatures stir, rivers gleam,
Afternoon whispers, old, yet new.

In this moment, brief and profound,
The moon and sun share sky and sea,
A dance where silence is the sound,
And time itself feels wild and free.

Silent Conversations

Beneath the stars, in quiet night,
The world is hushed, no need for words,
The moon converses, soft and light,
With shadows cast by distant herds.

The trees, they sway and share their tales,
In whispers carried by the breeze,
In silence, every leaf prevails,
To paint the calm with autumn leaves.

A river flows, its voice subdued,
Its secrets kept within the stream,
Conversations fluid, nude,
Reflections of a tranquil dream.

Through silent streets, the echoes weave,
A story of the night's embrace,
Each window lit, a soul believes,
In gentle night's forgiving grace.

In quietude, we find our peace,
The heart can speak without a sound,
In silent conversations cease,
To search, for here, true love is found.

Dreamer's Soliloquy

In the realm where shadows play,
A dreamer rises from the deep,
With eyes that pierce the close of day,
And secrets that the heart will keep.

Amidst the veil of twilight's glow,
A soliloquy of stars unfolds,
Each stanza whispers soft and low,
A universe of tales retold.

In dreams, the boundaries dissolve,
Reality, a fleeting ghost,
In slumber's arms, all problems solve,
And night becomes a gracious host.

The dreamer speaks in silent rhyme,
To moon and stars, a solemn plea,
A dance with fate, defying time,
Eternal quest for what could be.

When morning comes, the spells disperse,
The dreamer wakes with eyes anew,
But in the heart, the secret verse,
Of night's own soliloquy, true.

Midnight Echoes

In the hush of twilight's embrace,
Whispers travel through time and space,
Shadows dance upon the wall,
Midnight echoes softly call.

Silent streets and glowing moon,
A night's symphony, an ancient tune,
Leaves rustle, secrets confide,
In the dark, where dreams reside.

Owls hoot in distant trees,
A serenade carried by the breeze,
Stars align in cosmic show,
Under the sky, our spirits grow.

Lantern's glow flickers and fades,
In the magic that night's veil trades,
Whispers and echoes, ethereal play,
Carrying musings till break of day.

Between the lines of shadow and light,
The world transforms in the still of night,
As midnight whispers weave their threads,
Enchanted tales, where slumbers spread.

Wisdom After Dark

Moonlight spills on ancient stone,
Wisdom whispers when we're alone,
Night reveals what day conceals,
In darkness, old wounds can heal.

Quiet moments, thoughts unfold,
Stories of the wise retold,
Stars above like ancient tomes,
Guiding us to distant homes.

Mystic shadows, silent lore,
Lessons from the night-time shore,
Seek the truth in evening's song,
In twilight's arms, we all belong.

A symphony of crickets plays,
Guiding through the nocturnal maze,
Beyond the stars, a boundless sea,
Wisdom calls in the night's decree.

Darkness offers solace sweet,
In the night, our souls we meet,
Bound by lessons, old and bright,
Wisdom deepens in the night.

Lunar Reverie

Under the moon's gentle light,
Dreams awaken in the night,
Silver beams that touch the soul,
Glimmering tales yet to be told.

A quiet lake mirrors the sky,
Whispers of the night float by,
Ripples dance, stars take flight,
In lunar fields, hearts ignite.

Soft and still, a calm embrace,
In moon's glow we find our place,
Silent thoughts, moonlit streams,
Flow through our midnight dreams.

Phantoms wade in beams so thin,
In lunar reverie, dreams begin,
Night's soft blanket, tender kiss,
A tranquil moment, perfect bliss.

Hushed with care, the world sleeps tight,
Underneath the soft, glowing light,
Lunar whispers through the air,
In this reverie, we share.

Ode to the Stars

Above the world, in skies so vast,
Stars remind us of our past,
Glimmering points in the night,
Whispers of eternal light.

Constellations paint the sky,
Silent watchers, oh so high,
Guiding sailors through the seas,
Guardians of our destinies.

In the dark, their fires blaze,
Stories told in ageless ways,
Ancient beacons, blazing bright,
A symphony of starry light.

Cosmic dance of light and shade,
Timeless beauty, never fade,
Stars, you sing a lullaby,
To the earth and to the sky.

Eyes cast upward, hearts entwine,
With the stars, our souls align,
In your glow, we find our way,
Ode to stars, night's grand display.

Secrets of the Twilight

In twilight's soft embrace, we find
The whispers of a shadowed mind
A world between both day and night
Where secrets linger, out of sight

The amber glow, a fleeting kiss
Of sun and moon in tender bliss
Hidden truths in shades obscure
In twilight's hues, they do endure

Soft murmurs ride the evening breeze
Among the swaying, whispering trees
Nature's secrets, half-revealed
In twilight's shroud, forever sealed

The world's a canvas, softly drawn
Awakening to night from dawn
In twilight's arms, we gently sway
Where secrets hide and shadows play

A time of dreams, when hearts align
In twilight's hush, the stars will shine
And in this realm, so softly bright
We seek the secrets of the twilight

Dreams Beneath the Stars

Beneath the stars, our dreams take flight
In velvet skies of endless night
A tapestry of cosmic light
Illuminates our silent plight

Each twinkling gem, a wish set free
A doorway to eternity
In dreams, we sail on starlit seas
To realms of endless fantasy

The whispers of the night bestow
A magic only dreams can know
In every star, a story lies
And in our hearts, a knowing sigh

In quiet moments, we explore
The dreams that life has left in store
Beneath the stars, we venture far
To places light and wonder are

Each night, the starry sky invites
A journey through the endless heights
In dreams beneath the stars, we find
A universe within our mind

In the Silken Night

In the silken night, we lose our way
In shadows deep where phantoms play
A world of whispers, soft and low
Where moonbeams cast a gentle glow

Mysteries weave the silent air
With every breath, a secret flair
The night, a cloak of velvet dark
On which the stars leave tender marks

The silken threads of midnight's weave
Entangle dreams we dare to leave
In darkened corners, hopes ignite
And dance like fireflies in flight

Beneath the moon's embracing light
We find a solace in the night
A silken peace that wraps us tight
In dreams that twinkle, pure and bright

In the silken night's embrace, we find
A world of magic, warmly kind
Where dreams and shadows softly blend
And endless night will never end

Midnight Reverie

In the hours of deepest night
When moon and stars are burning bright
A quiet calm descends, so free
We dive into our reverie

Midnight whispers through the trees
A symphony of nightly breeze
It carries tales of ancient lore
To dreamer's minds forevermore

In twilight's hush, the world stands still
Our thoughts, like rivers, softly spill
Into a sea of boundless dreams
Where nothing's ever as it seems

Each moment in this midnight trance
Beckons us to take a chance
To wander through a starry maze
And lose ourselves in cosmic haze

A midnight reverie unfolds
A story in the dark retold
In every dream, a truth we find
That echoes deep within the mind

Quiet Hours

In the stillness of the night,
Whispers weave through darkened air,
Stars align with gentle light,
Dreams and thoughts silently share.

Crickets serenade the moon,
Soft winds cradle whispered pleas,
In this quiet midnight tune,
Worlds unfold with subtle ease.

Time feels different in this hour,
Peaceful, calm, where worries rest,
Nature speaks with silent power,
In this quiet, we are blessed.

Midnight Revelations

When the clock strikes twelve so clear,
Shadows play with flickering light,
Moments once obscured draw near,
Truth revealed in deepest night.

Dreams awake with vivid hue,
Secrets whispered in the dark,
Midnight brings its wisdom true,
Scarring souls with gentle mark.

In the echoes of the past,
Voices lost are found once more,
Midnight paths where memories last,
Touching hearts to their core.

Lunar Secrets

Moonlight dances on the waves,
Casting silver on the sea,
In her glow, the dark she braves,
Revealing truths that set us free.

Shadows play with soft delight,
Guiding us through night's embrace,
Unveiling secrets cloaked in light,
In her glow, we find our place.

Softly whispers stars above,
Tales of ancient times and lore,
Through the night, they speak of love,
Lunar secrets we adore.

Twilight Contemplations

As the day fades into dusk,
Colors blend in twilight's hue,
Thoughts emerge from shadows' musk,
Dreams of what and dreams of who.

In the quiet of this time,
Reflecting on the day's advance,
Moments caught in silent rhyme,
Life's unfolding subtle dance.

Stars begin their nightly show,
Lighting paths for us to see,
In this twilight's gentle glow,
Contemplations set us free.

Mystic Hours

In shadow's calm, where whispers meet,
I walk on paths of dew and mist.
Stars above in silence greet,
A realm of dreams by moonlight kissed.

The night enfolds in tender grace,
A symphony of hushed delight.
Time itself begins to trace,
The dance of dusk and darkened light.

In mystic hours, souls set free,
To wander through a world unseen.
The heart finds peace, its quiet plea,
In moments caught between a dream.

Illusions weave through soft night air,
As constellations softly gleam.
A tapestry beyond compare,
The fabric of the night's sweet theme.

As dawn approaches, sighs are shared,
The secrets of the night confide.
In mystic hours, none are scared,
To let their truest selves reside.

Embrace of Twilight

The sky's embrace of twilight's hue,
A canvas brushed with shades of peace.
Soft whispers float on breezes new,
As day begins its slow release.

In amber light, the world unwinds,
The echo of the day subsides.
The evening breathes in subtle signs,
Of dreams where hidden hope resides.

Each shadow lengthens, gently leans,
To cradle earth in tender might.
The world drifts softly into dreams,
Within the arms of coming night.

Nature's hush, a tender touch,
Of twilight's whispered, sweet retreat.
Time itself gives pause as such,
To offer night a gentle seat.

In twilight's calm, we find the grace,
To cast aside the day's demands.
And in its tender, warm embrace,
We hold our dreams within our hands.

Silhouettes in Starlight

Beneath the vast and endless sky,
Where stardust weaves its twinkling glow.
Silhouettes in starlight lie,
A dance of dreams that softly flow.

The night unfolds with cosmic grace,
Illumined by a distant light.
Each star a point in endless space,
A guide through corridors of night.

In stillness marked by heaven's beams,
We trace the patterns of the stars.
Lost within our quiet dreams,
Of worlds untouched by earthly scars.

The silhouettes against the night,
In silent tales, their stories weave.
A timeless scroll of purest light,
In starlight's embrace, we believe.

As night matures, its secrets shared,
We listen to the stars' soft song.
Silhouettes in starlight bared,
Remind us where our dreams belong.

Nocturnal Narratives

The night exhales its whispered lore,
In rhythmic breeze and cricket's call.
A gentle sigh from ancient store,
Of stories sung as shadows fall.

Beneath the moon's soft, tender gaze,
Nocturnal tales begin to weave.
The night's embrace, a velvet haze,
In which our hearts choose to believe.

Each whisper on the midnight air,
A narrative, both old and new.
Of love and loss, beyond compare,
Where time itself dissolves from view.

In every rustle, every sigh,
The night reveals its hidden prose.
Beneath the depth of starry sky,
The saga of the darkness flows.

Nocturnal narratives unfold,
In silence rich with meaning deep.
As fleeting moments, tales of old,
Become the dreams we long to keep.

Whispers of the Void

In the silence beyond sight,
Where shadows blend and fade,
Lie whispers of the night,
In the void, unafraid.

Stars adorn the blackened skies,
Their light a fleeting song,
Whispers dance, a soft reprise,
Where timeless echoes throng.

From depths unknown they call,
A lullaby of dreams,
Through the void's endless hall,
Where reality redeems.

In the still and quiet air,
Secrets softly glide,
Whispers weave a silver snare,
In the void, they hide.

Unseen forces gently steer,
Through realms of light and shade,
Whispers of the void draw near,
In silence, unafraid.

Illuminated Silence

In the glow of twilight's fall,
Silence whispers soft and clear,
Illuminated through it all,
Light and shadows, ever near.

Quiet lingers like a breeze,
Through the trees it softly flows,
Linking moments, bound with ease,
In this hush, the silence grows.

Candles flicker in the night,
Casting shadows, drawing near,
In their flame a silent light,
Speaks the words we long to hear.

In the heart of stillness found,
Illuminated rays collide,
Silent echoes all around,
In this peace, our fears subside.

Harmony of quiet dreams,
Illuminated by a glow,
In the silence, be it seems,
Truth and light forever flow.

Echoes Beneath the Stars

Underneath a sky so vast,
Echoes murmur in the night,
From the distant, ancient past,
Guiding with their tender light.

Stars above in endless span,
Whisper tales of yesteryear,
Echoes carry where they can,
Songs of joy, and words of fear.

Through the night, their voices rise,
Carried by the cosmic breeze,
Echoes weave through starlit skies,
In a dance of timeless ease.

Beneath the stars, dreams unfold,
In the echoes, we reside,
Stories new and tales old,
Cross the heavens, far and wide.

In the stillness, voices speak,
Softly calling from afar,
Echoes drifting as we seek,
Magic beneath every star.

Reflections at Dusk

As the sun begins to set,
And the night prepares its veil,
Reflections cast with no regret,
In the dusk, our hearts inhale.

Shadows stretch across the land,
Colors blend in twilight's hue,
Reflections meet by nature's hand,
As the world bids day adieu.

In the quiet of the eve,
Whispers of the day align,
Reflections start as dreams weave,
In the dusk, our thoughts entwine.

Moments caught between the beams,
Of the sun's last fleeting light,
Reflections flow like drifting streams,
Guiding souls into the night.

Peace descends in gentle waves,
Dusk wraps all in soft embrace,
Reflections of the day it saves,
As the stars take their place.

Solitude at Dusk

Upon the horizon, day's end whispers low,
A canvas of amber where shadows grow.
Silent as the breeze, the evening sways,
In solitude's embrace, the heart obeys.

The twilight beckons with a gentle sigh,
Echoes of the sun bid the sky goodbye.
Stars emerge in clusters, a night parade,
In the quiet dusk, all troubles fade.

Crickets compose symphonies from the dark,
Orchestrating night's serene embark.
An owl hoots softly, wisdom on wings,
In solitude at dusk, the soul sings.

Reflections dance upon the water's face,
Time momentarily loses its trace.
The world retreats into night's careful grasp,
Solitude at dusk ever so vast.

A crescent moon ascends the quiet night,
Guiding the wanderer by soft moonlight.
Dreams awaken in the gentle hush,
In solitude at dusk, a tranquil rush.

Voices in the Still

Whispers linger within the quiet night,
Echoes of stories in the soft moonlight.
The still air hums with secrets untold,
Voices in silence, a tale unfolds.

Shadows converse with the sleeping earth,
In stillness, they find their worth.
Winds carry murmurs from distant seas,
Voices in the still, a gentle tease.

The forest breathes with an ancient tongue,
Leaves rustle with songs unsung.
Beneath the canopy, whispers thrill,
Echoes of life, voices in the still.

Starlight weaves through the night's dark veil,
Telling tales with a silvered trail.
Each twinkle a word, each silence a thrill,
The language of night, voices in the still.

Hush now, listen to the silence speak,
In the quiet, we find what we seek.
In the lull of night, our souls fill,
With whispered truths, voices in the still.

Cryptic Darkness

An eerie calm falls with the night,
Shadows dance in the dim moonlight.
Cryptic whispers float on the breeze,
Secrets hidden among the trees.

The darkness wraps the world in its shroud,
Stars pierce the cloak like diamonds proud.
Ominous shapes among the gloom,
In the cryptic dark, mysteries loom.

Footsteps echo on the ancient path,
Guided only by the night's cold breath.
Each step a journey into the unknown,
In cryptic darkness, we walk alone.

Whispers of past and future entwine,
In the night's embrace, the soul resigns.
Cryptic truths emerge in midnight's hold,
Silent stories yearning to be told.

The night unveils its hidden lore,
In shadows deep, we explore.
Cryptic darkness, an enigma vast,
Whispering secrets from the past.

Twilight Meditations

As day retreats, twilight comes to roam,
Bringing tranquility far from home.
Thoughts start to wander in the fading light,
Twilight meditations, quiet and bright.

The sky blushes with the setting sun,
A tranquil end to a day well done.
In the gentle glow, the mind unwinds,
Twilight meditations, peace it finds.

Stars appear like distant dreams,
In twilight's embrace, the soul redeems.
Soft whispers of a world at ease,
Twilight meditations, moments to seize.

The night approaches with a gentle grace,
Dreams and reality intertwine in space.
In twilight's pause, all fears dissolve,
Twilight meditations, heart and soul evolve.

As the day yields to night's tender call,
In the twilight's hush, we find it all.
A time for thought, a time for dreams,
Twilight meditations, life's twilight gleams.

After Hours Thoughts

In the stillness of the night,
Where silence whispers softly.
Dreams take flight, a quiet delight,
In a world where thoughts are lofty.

Stars like memories, brightly forged,
Flicker in the vast, dark sky.
Questions form, then gently gorge,
And through the mind, they drift and fly.

Night unveils the hidden fears,
In the heart's most secret spaces.
Unseen, the journey through the years,
Leaves behind the faintest traces.

Peace then dances on the breeze,
Mingling with the soft moonlight.
In the calm, the soul finds ease,
In the deep and tranquil night.

Wisdom gathers, moment gleams,
In this quiet, sacred hour.
In the realm of midnight dreams,
Thoughts emerge with gentle power.

Veil of Darkness

Shadows fall, the day's retreat,
Night's embrace is calm and tender.
Footsteps marked by echo's beat,
Darkness, yet a silent splendor.

Whispers form in hidden nooks,
Winds that sweep through ancient sighs.
Mysteries locked in secret books,
Caught beneath the inky skies.

Curtains drawn on twilight's stage,
Stars as actors, soft and bright.
Moonlight writes on life's dark page,
Scripted tales in silver light.

Dreams awake in starlit shroud,
Hearts enlivened by the dawn.
Truths emerge from night's dark cloud,
Revealing where the soul is drawn.

Night reveals what light conceals,
In its veil, our truth divines.
In the dark, the heart reveals,
Wisdom found between the lines.

Wonders of the Midnight Mind

Deep within the quiet night,
Dreams unfurl on midnight's breeze.
Thoughts arise, a silent flight,
In the still, the mind finds ease.

Stars above in endless sprawl,
Lighting paths through boundless skies.
Whispers call, a siren's drawl,
Leading where the insight lies.

Luna's glow on shadows cast,
Illuminates the searching soul.
Mysteries of future, past,
In the dark, unite and toll.

Nighttime thoughts in silence blend,
Conscious streams in quiet flow.
Untold tales they downward send,
Secrets of the heart bestow.

In the quiet, wisdom found,
Lies unveiled in tender light.
Awakened dreams without a sound,
Wonders of the midnight night.

Crescent Dreams

Moonlight in its crescent phase,
Casts a gentle, silken glow.
Dreams arise from hidden bays,
Like the tides in ebb and flow.

Silent whispers dance on air,
In the stillness of the dawn.
Nighttime holds a heartfelt prayer,
To the light that greets the morn.

Stars above in quiet dance,
Sparkle with a mystic gleam.
In their glow, the mind's expanse,
Weaves the fabric of each dream.

Silent musings softly tread,
On the pathways of the night.
Crescent dreams where souls are led,
Towards the dawn's awaiting light.

In the calm where shadows blend,
Wisdom flows through lunar beams.
Night's embrace, a soothing friend,
Guiding softly, crescent dreams.

Darker Than Dreams

In shadows deep, where secrets creep,
The moonlight fades, in silence weep.
A whisper cold, a tale untold,
In twilight's grasp, the night unfolds.

Stars wink from skies, with unseen eyes,
Where hope retreats, and sorrow flies.
Beneath the gloom, in nature's loom,
Is darkness spun, in spectral room.

Through forest dense, with spirits tense,
Dreams dissolve, where night commence.
In quiet dread, the fears we shed,
Upon this path, where none have tread.

With sombre sighs, the dawn defies,
The dreams once bright, now blackened lies.
A canvas stark, where shadows mark,
The heart's lament, in void so dark.

Yet in this night, devoid of light,
A soul may rise, from fearful plight.
For in the deep, where dark things keep,
Resilience grows, courage to reap.

Arc of Midnight

Through velvet skies, with milky light,
The stars align, in arc of night.
A cosmic bridge, on heaven's ridge,
In silent grace, they burn so bright.

From dusk till dawn, where shadows yawn,
The night unveils its mystic crown.
In silver streak, where dreamers seek,
A realm of peace, in silence bound.

The midnight's veil, in whispers frail,
Conceals the tales of ages pale.
Through fleeting beams, and stardust seams,
The night unfolds its ancient dreams.

With time asleep, the secrets keep,
In hallowed depths, where shadows seep.
A path unknown, with stars bestrown,
Marks heaven's arc, in silence steep.

Amidst the stars, with whispered scars,
The night invites, with open arms.
To dreamers true, the cosmos blue,
Bestows its light, in steadfast charms.

Radiant Stillness

In quiet dawn, where shadows shun,
The light returns, a rising sun.
A silent glow, where dreams bestow,
A gentle warmth, on hearts undone.

The morning air, with crisp declare,
Whispers soft, in tranquil care.
Each dewdrop bright, in morning light,
Reflects the day, with hope to share.

In silence pure, where hearts endure,
The world awakes, in calm allure.
A gentle peace, where stress may cease,
Bestows its grace, with touch demure.

Through stillness vast, the moments passed,
In quietude, a spell is cast.
A radiant calm, a morning psalm,
Inscribes its mark, where shadows fast.

As day ascends, with light amends,
The stillness blends, where nature tends.
A radiant thread, where silence led,
Unveils the morn, as night descends.

Quiet Nocturne

The night sighs deep, in realm of sleep,
Where dreams arise, and shadows creep.
A stillness great, within night's gate,
Enfolds the earth, where secrets keep.

Moon's tender light, in silver plight,
Illuminates the silent night.
A gentle song, where winds belong,
Weaves through the dark, with whispers slight.

The stars above, in skies of love,
Bestow their glow, from realms above.
In quiet hue, where night is true,
Their radiance speaks, in gentle shove.

Through night's embrace, in silent space,
A calm descends, with tender grace.
A symphony, where hearts agree,
Finds solace there, in night's embrace.

With dawn's return, where shadows burn,
The night's quietude does adjourn.
Yet hearts recall, the night's soft thrall,
In memories, where dreams still yearn.

Moonlit Whispers

In the velvet hush of night,
The moonbeams softly play,
Silver threads of quiet light,
Weave through shadows' sway.

Whispers drift on gentle breeze,
Secrets shared with muted trees,
Silent tales of ancient seas,
Echo in the night's deep freeze.

Stars align like stories told,
Constellations brave and bold,
In their splendor, dreams unfold,
Whispers of a world grown old.

Moonlit paths through meadows wide,
In their glow, our fears subside,
There, where night and peace collide,
Lonely hearts find hope inside.

Through the dark, a guiding beam,
Whispered secrets softly teem,
In the moon's enchanting gleam,
We are lost within a dream.

Starlit Reflections

Under skies with diamonds spread,
Reflections of the worlds above,
Glistening dreams in cosmic thread,
Tales of ancient, distant love.

Mirrored in the darkened sea,
Stars reveal what we could be,
Infinite in mystery,
Starlit whispers set us free.

Echoes of the long-lost past,
In their silence, shadows cast,
Moments held but fleeting fast,
Glories seen through midnight's blast.

Constellations pause in space,
Hearts aligned in quiet grace,
Each bright spark in time's embrace,
Bids us join this celestial race.

In these stars, we find our fate,
Dreams ignite, our hearts elate,
Starlit visions captivate,
Guiding us through heaven's gate.

Echoes After Dark

When the twilight bids adieu,
Night's embrace comes softly near,
Echoes form in shades of blue,
Stirring memories held dear.

Footsteps in the silent lane,
Ghostly whispers call in vain,
Mysteries they can't explain,
Twilight's echo, subtle, plain.

Olden songs dance in the air,
Lost in time, beyond compare,
In the dark, emotions flare,
Whispering a silent prayer.

Echoes of a lover's sigh,
In the night, hearts cannot lie,
Underneath the star-filled sky,
These soft echoes amplify.

Darkness holds a hidden lore,
Echoes of the yesteryore,
Through the night, they gently soar,
Guiding us forevermore.

Nocturnal Musings

In the quiet of the night,
Thoughts take flight and dreams ignite,
Wonders hidden from our sight,
Dance amidst the twinkling light.

Through the silence, moments gleam,
Like reflections in a stream,
Midnight's canvas, pure and clean,
Holds the dreams that we redeem.

Wisdom of the night unfolds,
In the dark, new stories told,
Silent secrets, brave and bold,
Cast from legends, bright and old.

Nocturnal whispers gently sing,
Joy and sorrow on the wing,
In their hold, new hopes they bring,
Like the promise of the spring.

In the quiet of the night,
Find your truth in shadows slight,
With the dawn, hearts reunite,
Guided by the moon's soft light.

The Waking Stillness

Morning whispers in quiet tones,
A silent symphony sings alone.
Dewdrops glisten, soft and clear,
Awakening the world, drawing near.

The hush of dawn, pure and bright,
Soft shadows chase the fleeing night.
Birdsongs weave a gentle lace,
Each note a kiss, a warm embrace.

Trees stand tall in reverent grace,
Sunlight paints every solemn face.
Fragile leaves in breezes play,
Heralding the break of day.

In this moment, time stands still,
As nature's pulse begins to thrill.
The waking stillness, deep and wise,
Greets the new day with open eyes.

Through the Night's Veil

Soft whispers in the moonlit haze,
Glimmers of a spectral maze.
Dreamlike visions come to play,
As shadows dance the night away.

Velvet veils embrace the sky,
Stars like diamonds, twinkling high.
Through the night, a silent grace,
Time and space begin to chase.

Mystery lurks in every breeze,
Whispers carried through the trees.
Night's embrace is deep and wide,
Guiding dreams with every tide.

Moments blend in twilight's spell,
Under night's dark, gentle shell.
Through the veil, we gently drift,
In its fold, sweet dreams we lift.

Luminous Thoughts

Bright ideas in shadows born,
Twinkling lights before the morn.
Mind and soul in cosmic dance,
Guided by a fleeting chance.

Luminous thoughts like fireflies,
Illuminate the darkened skies.
Visions of tomorrow gleam,
Woven from the heart's pure dream.

Ephemeral, yet bright they burn,
Twisting, turning at every turn.
In the quiet of the mind,
Precious gems are there to find.

In the silence, light shall grow,
Thoughts in endless patterns flow.
A universe within our sight,
With every thought, a spark of light.

Wisdom in the Shadows

In shadows deep, where secrets lie,
The ancient whispers softly sigh,
A tapestry of time unfolds,
With stories wise and truths untold.

Within the twilight's gentle grip,
Lessons learned from night's own lips,
Subtle echoes guide our way,
Through hidden paths both night and day.

Underneath the moonlit veil,
Wisdom in shadows, none can pale,
Mysteries of the heart and mind,
And treasures only few shall find.

Darkness speaks in silent tones,
The wisdom that the night has sown,
An artful dance of light's embrace,
In shadows find your destined place.

Embrace the dusk, the quiet hue,
The night is old but always new,
For in the depths where shadows dwell,
Lies wisdom with a tale to tell.

Whispers of the Dark

The night winds sing a ghostly song,
Where spirits dance and shadows long,
The starlit skies divulge each arc,
In whispers of the velvety dark.

Beneath the cloak of midnight's sway,
Soft voices call in mystic play,
From realms unseen, their secrets spark,
In whispers of the dusky dark.

A lullaby from times gone by,
Hums through the night, a gentle cry,
An age-old message leaves its mark,
In whispers of the silent dark.

Horizon fades, the world stands still,
A haunting tune, a soulful thrill,
In twilight's grasp, the night embarks,
On whispers soft, serene, and stark.

Let shadows speak their tender lore,
Of whispered dreams forevermore,
The stories old that legends hark,
In whispers of the endless dark.

Luminous Thoughts

In the quiet mind where dreams alight,
Luminous thoughts take silent flight,
A symphony of boundless light,
Guiding souls through endless night.

Amidst the calm of inner peace,
Shining whispers ever cease,
To still the storm, to ease the plight,
With luminous thoughts so pure and bright.

Reflections in a sea of calm,
Illuminate the spirit's psalm,
A guiding star in darkest plight,
With luminous thoughts as pure as light.

Enlightened whispers gently breathe,
The essence of the skies beneath,
A gentle glow, a silent might,
With luminous thoughts, hearts unite.

In the realm of silent dreams,
Where nothing's ever as it seems,
Find the glow that sparks the night,
In luminous thoughts, our souls take flight.

Dreamer's Lament

In the stillness of the night,
Dreams take wing, a fleeting sight,
A whisper in the moon's lament,
The dreamer's heart is gently spent.

Beneath the stars, a quiet sigh,
As dreams cascade across the sky,
A silent tear, a wish unpent,
The dreamer's soul in deep descent.

Through fields of thought, the mind does roam,
In search of light, in search of home,
The weight of dreams, a heart's intent,
Becomes the dreamer's true lament.

Hopes and fears, a tangled dance,
In sleep's embrace, a fleeting glance,
With every dawn, a night well-spent,
The echoes of the dreamer's lament.

Though dreams may fade with morning's light,
They linger on through day and night,
An endless song, an ever-present,
The timeless tune of dreamer's lament.

Whispers of the Celestial Dome

Beneath the vault of endless blue,
Where dreams and stardust gently strew,
Celestial whispers softly roam,
In twilight's hush, they call us home.

Through cosmic veils, the night unfolds,
Enigmas wrapped in stories old,
Stars trace a path in silent roam,
The sky, a layered, deep tome.

Nebulas weave through tales untold,
Mysteries written in skies of gold,
Comets streak and planets dwell,
In vast expanse, our hearts compel.

Luna's glow on earth below,
A dance of shadows, ebb, and flow,
Galaxies blend in color's foam,
We gaze aloft, on time we comb.

Each twinkling light, a distant hymn,
Across the heavens, bright and dim,
Feel the pull, the welcome tone,
In whispers of the celestial dome.

Shadows of Sleep

As twilight fades to velvet night,
In realms of dreams and soft moonlight,
A hush descends, the shadows creep,
Inviting all to twilight's keep.

Whispers blend with silence lush,
A world in muted, ambient hush,
Figures dance in mystic sweep,
Enveloped in the shadows of sleep.

Lost in folds of darkened hues,
We wander realms of twilight cues,
Beyond the veils, our spirits leap,
In midnight's grasp, the shadows seep.

Each breath a lull of night's embrace,
As dreams begin their tender chase,
The mind, it dives in tranquil deep,
Beneath the cloak of shadows steep.

Till dawn breaks with gentle nudge,
Dispelling night with warming budge,
From shadows' clasp, we gently creep,
Renewed from realms of slumber's keep.

Midnight Reverberations

In the quiet of the midnight air,
Whispers travel, pure and rare,
Echoes bounce off moonlit stones,
Midnight's song in rhythmic tones.

Through the still, the echoes glide,
A symphony, the stars confide,
Soundless chords, yet deep proclamations,
In the pulse of night's vibrations.

Winds weave tales in subtle tunes,
Through shadows cast by silver moons,
Night itself a grand oration,
Songs of old in reverberation.

Hearts attune to cosmic sound,
In silence, hidden songs are found,
Each note a pure, sweet revelation,
Harmonics of the midnight's vibrations.

Till morning breaks the silence pure,
The night recedes, its echoes cure,
Yet in our minds, those constellations,
Stay bright with midnight reverberations.

Moonlit Insights

Bathed in silver, the night unfurls,
Moonlight brushing soft on pearls,
Whispers carried on a breeze,
With moonlit insights, hearts find ease.

In solitude, where shadows play,
Thoughts find wings, and doubts allay,
The mind reflects, as night reveals,
In moonlit glow, the soul it heals.

Paths once hidden, now adorned,
By beams of Luna, softly warmed,
Every glisten, insights bloom,
In the still of night's soft room.

The world in hush, yet speaks so clear,
With moonlit truths, it draws us near,
Glimpses of a time unfeared,
In gentle light, our hearts are steered.

Till morning sweeps those beams away,
And dawn unfurls its warmer sway,
Still, in our minds, those lunar sights,
Alive with guide in moonlit insights.